The 100-Hour Pilot: Fulfilling a Lifelong Dream

Brian Brogen

ISBN Number: 979-8625074933

DEDICATION

To my darling wife, Jennifer Brogen, who was patient with me and encouraged me to fulfill this dream. To my children, who tolerate the constant talk of flying and the occasional distraction of a passing airplane. To my Mom, who instilled courage in me and taught me my favorite Bible memory verse, Philippians 4:13 - I can do all things through Christ, which strengthens me! To my Dad, who gave me my love of and care for others. He has never met a stranger and would truly give you the shirt off his back. To all of my family and friends who have supported me in my life. To all current and future aviators.

CONTENTS

ACKNOWLEDGMENTS

I would like to thank my instructor, Jim Porterfield, and the other instructors who helped me with lessons on flying. A very special thank you to Mack Story, for strongly encouraging me to write a book and helping me format this book. I would also like to thank my Mom, Cindy Cochran, for the countless hours she spent proofreading and editing this book.

DISCLAIMER

This book was written for entertainment and is not to be used as flight instruction. Remember, I am an amateur, 100-hour pilot. I don't claim to be an expert. I am sure I will make some errors in my descriptions and ask for your understanding in advance. If you have questions, please consult your flight instructor for their professional instruction.

1

THE STUDENT

Passion Ignites

Growing up, I always dreamed of becoming a pilot. At nine years old, after watching an aerobatic pilot overhead from my front yard one day, I remember running into the house with great excitement to tell my parents about the airplane.

After watching the hit movie Top Gun (1986) as a preteen, I decided I wanted to be a fighter pilot like "Maverick," played by Tom Cruise. The flying was phenomenal and the dogfights (aerial battles) were mesmerizing. It was such a hit the United States Navy had a surge in young people wanting to join the Navy and become naval aviators. Everyone – myself included - wanted a bomber jacket and a pair of aviator sunglasses like the pilots wore in the film.

When I was 12 years old, my mom enrolled me in the Civil Air Patrol Cadet Program, where I learned about aviation and got to fly in my first general aviation airplane. The airplane was the ever-popular Cessna 172. They even let me briefly take the controls and fly! I was hooked.

Interestingly, years later, as an adult, I decided to look up the tail number of that airplane, which I gathered from the photos my mom took on the day of my discovery flight. I found out the airplane was in an accident a few years after my flight. This was a sobering moment for me, especially since I was pursuing my pilot license at the time. The airplane was reportedly a total loss, and the pilot and Civil Air Patrol cadet were seriously injured.

But back then as a teenager, I was filled with hope and little fear, and had a plan to go to the Air Force Academy to become a fighter pilot. I wanted to serve 20 years, then retire from the military and become a commercial airline pilot.

The Dream, Reimagined

As it goes for many young people, my plans didn't quite work out. My parents divorced when I was 14 and I became rebellious, defiant, and lashed out at both of them to the extent that separation was necessary at times. At one point, I asked my mother to place me in a youth shelter because I didn't want to live with either parent.

This was a difficult period in my life. Although the

youth home was advertised on television with a summer camp feel, touting climbing walls, a rope course, etc., I never experienced those extracurricular activities. I shared a room with a teenage car thief and there was even a fellow teen who had been accused of attempted murder. One of these teenagers spent a few hours in the "rubber room" banging his body and head into the walls.

The situation was scary for a young man who was raised in a suburban home and missed very few Sunday school classes. I made sure to be on best behavior; time out in a "rubber room" was no place for me. Many of these teens were in the shelter on court orders, rather than like me, who chose to be there.

Although my home was uncomfortable at times, both my parents loved me. My situation paled in comparison to most of the other teenagers. I soon came to realize I really didn't belong in this environment. After several weeks, my Mom welcomed me back home. That is the closest I have been to being locked up and I never want to experience it again.

There was some time for self-reflection during my stay at the shelter and I came away appreciating what I had been blessed with and resolved to make a better life. After I left the youth shelter, I bounced back and forth between my parents and attended five different high schools. I barely met the requirements to graduate from high school, and ultimately had to perform community service to get the last few required credits. At the time, I hated school, so I was glad to finally be finished.

Something I did always enjoy, perhaps paradoxically, was working. My dad had a lawn service and when I was around 12 years old, I remember him bragging to my mother about how hard I had worked weed eating while he mowed during the summer.

After graduating high school, without plans for college or a defined path into the military, I needed a job. The family of some friends of mine owned a steel fabrication and construction company. Though I was only looking for a job, I was fortunate enough to find a rewarding career.

In my 25 years at Southeastern Construction and Maintenance, I have never "called in sick." I'm pleased to say I have perfect attendance, something I didn't even strive for in school.

While growing my career, I also devoted time to growing my family: my wife and I have four children (Brittney, James, Matthew and Rebecca). Given the responsibilities of raising a family, affording a pilot's license wasn't even on my radar for quite a while.

Although I would still talk about my dream to friends and had several supporters encourage me to make it happen, it just wasn't an option financially. The boys are twins and whoever came up with the saying "two for the price of one" has never bought formula, diapers, food, and clothing for two babies. Our children are worth more than anything, and they were, and continue to be, my top priority. My dreams of soaring through the sky would remain on hold.

I would occasionally stop in an airport and discuss flight training and bring the paperwork home. After calculating the expense, however, I resolved to just keep dreaming.

Between 2003-2015, I obtained a general contractor's license in Florida, Georgia, and Alabama, a roofing license in Florida, and a Project Management Professional designation. These qualifications enabled me to be more productive to my employer, and thus earn higher wages.

I also established a side hustle using my experience and qualifications to help others and to keep up with the growing financial needs of my family. Although I am not rich in the financial sense, I learned the value of savings and investments, and made them work for me and my aspirations as a husband, father, employee, and businessman.

Success on the Horizon

As my 40th birthday approached, I once again stopped by the airport to see what flight training cost in 2016. When I calculated the expense this time, I finally felt I could afford it. I discussed my desires with my wife and, to my utter amazement and absolute excitement, she agreed I should pursue this enduring goal. Yay!

Now, my dear wife has always accused me of being color blind, a potential hurdle in my pursuit of piloting. To her credit, I have certainly made incorrect assessments of the color of other people's clothing and called shirts or pants incorrect colors. Through some quality control training on my job, I took the Ishihara color blind test and discovered she was right (again!).

Despite my diagnosed colorblindness, I got right to work completing the requirements, and I successfully completed my first solo flight before turning 40, and got my license a few months later. I had finally fulfilled my lifelong ambition!

I made the Aviation Medical Examiner (AME), an FAA-designated doctor, aware I am color blind. Though I passed the aviation medical exam, I was restricted to day flight. Upon further research, I learned there was a signal light test administered by the Federal Aviation Administration (FAA) and, if passed, the day flight restriction can be removed. I scheduled and passed, allowing me to fly at night. So fear not, my fellow color-challenged friends – there is still hope for night flying!

Sharing the Success

My twin boys tease me that becoming a pilot was a mid-life crisis. Maybe it was, but I still enjoy it like a kid.

So, for me, the student pilot was a 40-year-old man, wanting to obtain his pilot's license to fulfill a lifetime dream at (or near) a milestone birthday.

During my training, I met many other student pilots of varying ages, from the 16-year-olds who had obtained scholarships from the awesome

James C. Ray Foundation, to the 70-plus-year-old wanting to solo, and every age in between.

According to the FAA, to become a student pilot you must be at least 16 years of age and undergo a routine medical examination that must be administered by FAA AMEs.

Even if you have a physical handicap, like my color blindness, for instance, medical certificates can be issued in many cases. Operating limitations may be imposed depending upon the nature of the disability.

With this book, I hope to share the knowledge I have gained throughout the process, including my personal experience, to inspire others to follow their dream, regardless of age or any other perceived limitation. I firmly believe anyone with a passion for aviation can be a student pilot and attain their dream to fly!

2

THE AIRPLANE

A (Very) Brief Historical and Scientific Overview

It is an amazing craft with many names - flying machine, airplane, aeroplane, flying ship, seaplane, jet ... the list goes on and on. But just how did humans go about taking flight?

Famously, in 1903, the Wright Brothers made their first flight just south of Kitty Hawk, NC in the Wright Flyer. Between 1904-1905, the brothers developed their flying machine into the first practical fixed-wing aircraft, the Wright Flyer III.

Now, over a century later, there are an almost innumerable number of different types of planes with various rating or endorsement requirements for the pilots. Aside from their diversity, most airplanes are basically similar in that they have an engine, wings, and surface controls. All make use of Bernoulli's principle: air flows faster over the top of the wing and slower below the wing, creating lift.

My instructor liked to say the Americans got credit

for inventing the plane, but the French perfected the design. This is the reason some parts of the airplane have French names: fuselage, ailerons, empennage, pitot, etc.

An Array of Aircraft

There are varying aircraft types and categories corresponding to a craft's mission and the pilot's ratings/endorsements.

I am currently a Private Pilot Single Engine Land (ASEL). This is the most common license sought by private pilots, who cannot fly for hire or commercially. This license, like all pilot licenses, restricts and permits flight to certain types of aircraft.

As of this writing, I have had the privilege of flying both a Cessna 172 and a Piper PA-28. I took my instruction in a Cessna 172, and therefore have much more experience with it.

This is the Cessna 172 N5328Z used for my flight training.

The 172 is very popular in training and is one of the most readily available rental planes. If you begin flight training, you will most likely become familiar with a 172 or at least see many of them at the airport. The 172 is a high wing plane, which allows a great view for sightseeing below.

During your training, you will become very familiar with the airplane used during your instruction. You should consult the Pilot Operating Handbook to find out about the airplane you are flying and its performance.

An airplane-specific checklist will be used prior to

each flight and will ensure the plane is ready for flight. I can tell you from experience, it is pretty difficult to taxi with the tail of the plane tied to the ground! Be sure you use your checklist completely. Use of your checklist will prevent dumb (and embarrassing!) mistakes. It could also save your life. Many general aviation accidents could have been prevented with the strict adherence to a checklist.

During training, I mostly used the SP Skyhawk. This model has Lycoming IO-360-L2A powerplant (engine) that produces 180 horsepower.

My instructor would always say, "This thing loves to fly, and if airspeed isn't managed correctly, they will float while trying to land." Floating is a condition of landing with too much airspeed and the airplane still wants to fly. You can float down the runway too far and either miss the desired touchdown point or miss the opportunity for a safe landing.

Since obtaining my license, I have been flying a 172N Skyhawk. This model has a Lycoming O-320-H2AD powerplant that produces 160 horsepower. There is a noticeable difference in the power variance, but it flies almost identically to the

SP Skyhawk on which I trained.

I am hopeful to get some time in airplanes with a little more cruise speed so cross-country flights are more feasible. However, the C172 Skyhawk will always be my first love.

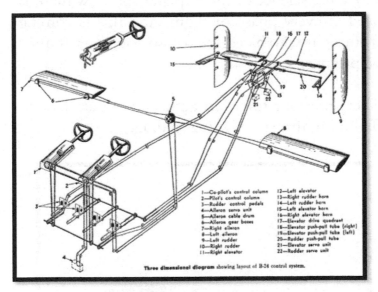

B24 Cable Control Diagram

As you can see in the illustration above, the cable wire-controlled system is very simple. Its classic design has not changed in many years.

I am amazed when I crawl through historic military planes on display at fly-ins and see the same controls as the small general aviation planes

I have flown. These historic planes, used to defend our freedom, have a design that is still relevant today!

Practical Math and Science

I love the science of the airplane and how math is used in every phase of flight (and this is coming from a guy who hated school, so you know it must be pretty engaging stuff!).

There are four forces in action on an airplane in flight: lift, thrust, weight, and drag.

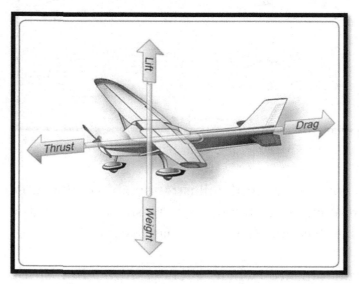

Lift opposes weight and is created by Bernoulli's Principle -- air flows faster over the top of the wing and slower underneath. Thrust is created by the powerplant and engine moving the plane in a forward motion. The weight is the gross weight of the plane, pilot, passengers, baggage and fuel. Drag is air pushing against the surface of the plane and creating a resistance to thrust.

During your training, you will learn how to perform weight and balance calculations to determine if the load is within the design parameters of the plane.

You will also learn what the center of gravity is and how to load an airplane to ensure it's balanced per the Pilot's Operating Handbook.

Most people (including myself, prior to training) are initially overwhelmed by the numerous gauges and switches in the panel. Once you understand how the "six pack," or the equivalent glass cockpit readings, work, you will understand there are very similar gauges in the dash of your car.

At times, I even find myself pretending to fly my truck with the use of the speedometer and tachometer. Sure, it's missing the vertical speed indicator, attitude indicator, altimeter, etc.; but, hey, we are pretending!

3

THE INSTRUCTOR

Who's Who When You're Sky High

A certified flight instructor (CFI) must hold at least a commercial pilot certificate or an airline transport certificate (ATP). Instructors are tested not only on their knowledge of flying and aircrafts, but also on the fundamentals of instruction itself.

Choosing the CFI will be one of the most important decisions in your pursuit of a pilot's license. I recommend you interview multiple CFIs and give consideration to their experience, their personality, and their availability.

You'll spend a minimum of 20 hours (most likely more, according to statistics) with them in very close quarters. You don't want to begin flight instruction with a CFI only to discover along the way you don't trust or get along with them!

Some CFIs are working on becoming commercial airline pilots. For these pilots, flight instruction is a stepping stone to gain the experience and required number of hours to meet airline minimum requirements. This practice is known in aviation as "building hours."

Other CFIs are former military or airline pilots who either enjoy instruction or are working on a second career. There are also CFIs who have made flight instruction their primary career and really enjoy teaching people to fly.

Selecting for Fit and Excellence

Again, you will want to consider their availability, especially when considering a CFI who is working on becoming an airline pilot. If they are near their minimum required hours, they may be headed to the airlines before you complete your training, and this would be at least an interruption and potentially a significant setback in your training while you and a new flight instructor get acquainted.

When you interview potential CFIs, find out how many other CFIs are on their team. An alternate instructor is a good resource in the event your primary instructor is not available when you have time for training. It's also great to get another perspective and different style of teaching occasionally during training.

I met with at least five different CFIs within 30 minutes of my home before making my final decision. I really had a great time with my flight instructor, Jim Porterfield (Bartow Air Base). We hit it off at our first meeting and were fast friends. We both like to cut up and have a good time, so I knew choosing him would mean my training would be both educational and fun.

Time Really Flies...

During training, when we hit turbulence, I would let out a "WOO-HOO!" Jim would imitate me and laugh. I also had a habit of taking my hand off the throttle lever and getting a "death grip" on the yoke during landings. Jim would remove my right hand from the yoke and place it back on the throttle control, where it belonged. (Note: it is critical to have control of the throttle so you can do a "go around" if necessary.) A "go around" is when a pilot determines the landing is potentially unsafe and decides not to land and make a loop around the pattern for another attempt at a safe landing.

After several instances of Jim removing my hand from the yoke, he jokingly accused me of liking to hold his hand. That solved the problem and now I always remember to keep my hand on the throttle control!

Jim and I certainly had a lot of fun flying. In fact, he transposed the old saying "time flies when you're having fun" to "time's fun when you're having flies."

A Lesson on Flight Lessons

It is important for you to take control of your training. You are working on becoming a pilot in control (PIC), so you should practice being a student in control. This is one regret I have from my training – not being more thorough in my goals for the training.

I was having so much fun flying and sightseeing, I wasn't keeping track of where I was in training. I was dependent upon my instructor to remember where we were with training, but I should have been keeping careful notes and developing my own learning objectives that followed the syllabus. I could have been proactive in my training, rather than reactive.

Even though I have already obtained my pilot's license, I still subscribe to AOPA Flight Training magazine. I have read numerous articles encouraging student pilots to make a plan for each individual lesson. I definitely see where having a plan would reduce the number of hours required to obtain a pilot's license.

Remember, every hour with an instructor costs money. Take responsibility to make this time effective toward your goal of becoming a private pilot. If you take control of your instruction, you won't suspect your instructor of using you to "build time." This is a common concern among student pilots, but if you are smart, you can achieve your goals while helping them achieve theirs. A true symbiotic relationship in the skies!

4

THE AIRPORT

In the early days of flying, any open field that was relatively flat sufficed for a place to land and could be used as a makeshift "airport." Popularized in the 1920s, barnstorming

> **Airport** *(noun)*: Area on land or water used or intended to be used for the landing and take-off of aircraft.

was a practice wherein pilots traveled to often-rural locations and performed acrobatic maneuvers to draw a crowd. They would land in the open fields (typically near barns, hence the name) and charge for passenger flights and an airshow.

After many accidents and tragedies early on, it became apparent there was a need to regulate civil aviation, and true airports began to be the norm. Airports, much like airplanes, come in many shapes and sizes, from military airbases to privately-owned grass strips, and everything in between.

Following the terrorist attacks on 9/11, airport security was tightened tremendously, and they became less accessible to the public. All public airports are now fenced in, and have stringent security requirements. Though it can seem intimidating, do not let these hurdles deter you from going to your local airport and meeting the flying community.

My Home Air Base

As mentioned earlier, I took my training at Bartow Municipal Airport abbreviated as KBOW. BOW is the official Airport Identifier of Bartow Municipal Airport and all US mainland airports have a K followed by their unique identifier.

Bartow Airport has a rich history. It was used to train pilots during World War II. Buzz Aldrin, one of the world's most famous astronauts, trained at what was then known as Bartow Airfield. There is an awesome museum at the airport (Bartow Air Base History Museum).

Many Florida airports besides the one in Bartow were chosen as training grounds for military pilots due to the warm weather and proximity to the gulf and ocean for over-water training maneuvers.

Currently, KBOW is a controlled airport from 0730 to 1730 EST, meaning it has a control tower with an air traffic controller controlling the airspace from 7:30 AM to 5:30 PM EST. After 1730, the airport becomes pilot-controlled.

A Word on Runways

Airport runways are numbered by their magnetic heading, or direction relative to magnetic north. At KBOW, there are three paved runways - 9/27Left and its parallel runway 9/27Right and 5/23. Runway 9 is a 090 directional heading (heading east). Runway 27, at the opposite end of the runway, is a 270 directional heading (heading west). Runway 5 is a 050 directional heading (heading northeast). Runway 23, at the opposite end of the runway, is a 230 directional heading (heading southwest).

Bartow Municipal Airport (KBOW)

For a student pilot, having three runways helps reduce pilot workload. Since there are two 9/27 runways, a right and a left, you can use the "practice runway" and not interfere with other airport traffic. There is also the 5/23 runway for varying winds to minimize the effects of crosswind.

One of the "geezers" (we will discuss geezers - a term of endearment from an old aviation book - in another chapter) complained he never got to practice crosswind landing because of the runway options at KBOW.

I didn't fully appreciate or understand his comment until flying out of Wauchula with a single 18/36 runway and finding out there is almost always an opportunity to practice crosswind landings. When there is only a single runway there are not options of other runways to make the best use of the wind. Wind blowing straight down the runway is the most optimal for control of the airplane. Proficiency in crosswind landings will make you a better pilot - just remember: more rudder.

Fantastic Flights

Every flight is exhilarating, but my most memorable flight to date was from Gatlinburg, TN KGKT to Sylva, NC 24A. 24A has a 60' x 3,210' asphalt runway built on top of a blasted mountain top.

I took this flight with an instructor. Winds were calm, so she had me land on the lower end of a sloping runway. When this is done, the plane is landing uphill and uses the slope to slow the plane. This is probably the closest thing to an aircraft carrier landing I will get to experience.

In addition to the interesting landing, this flight had a beautiful view of Cade's Cove, the Smoky Mountains, and Fontana Lake. It was on my 42nd birthday in October 2018, so the leaves were just beginning to change. The views were gorgeous and made quite an impression on me.

Venice, FL KVNC is another unique runway. The final for runway 5 is over the Gulf of Mexico. In December of 2016, during my training,

At a little over 100 hours, I have had the privilege of flying into or out of the following airports:

- Bartow, FL KBOW
- Concord, NC KJQF
- Crystal River, FL KCGC
- Gatlinburg, TN KGKT
- Jackson County Sylva, NC 24A
- Lakeland, FL KLAL
- Miami-Opa Locka, FL KOPF
- Ocala, FL KOCF
- Palmetto, FL 48X
- Punta Gorda, FL KPGD
- Sebastian, FL X26
- Sebring, FL KSEF
- Stuart, FL KSUA
- Venice, FL KVNC
- Wauchula, FL KCHN
- Winter Haven, FL KGIF

my instructor chose this for our night cross country to show me how open waters on a dark night can be a trap for Visual Flight Rules (VFR) pilots. Since the horizon is dark and the water is dark, there is no reference point to the earth to determine if the plane is flying level. This is called Spatial Disorientation. It can also occur when flying through clouds with no reference of the horizon.

I have had other interesting experiences as well, each one different and exciting. In October of 2016, in Concord, NC KJQF, I took flight instruction from a local instructor while on a business trip. He gave me some new pointers and we flew over Lake Norman and saw the Charlotte skyline from a distance. It was beautiful.

My first actual soft field takeoff and landing took place in May of 2017 at Palmetto 48X, a grass strip located south of Tampa. It definitely made me appreciate the soft field training I had done on an asphalt runway.

The fixed-base operator (FBO, or airport office) at 48X is managed by Tom. He is a one-man show who loves flying, but isn't a pilot. He has the fridge and freezer stocked with snacks for pilots to buy. You can get into a conversation with Tom and lose track of time.

My mom lives in Sebastian, FL. I wanted to get some instruction on beach flying to prepare for a solo trip there to visit and fly with her at a later date. She had planned to wait on me while I took the instruction, but the instructor actually allowed her to come along as a passenger during my training. Flying over the east coast of Florida low and slow was gorgeous! This was my first and (to date) only flight in a low wing Piper Warrior. The instructor also wanted to familiarize me with landing the Piper Warrior, so we did a few landings. This plane does not float like the Cessna 172, it is heavier in landing. One landing was good, the second was firm.

I am finally learning when you have the power pulled, the plane is going to land. Keep it off the runway as long as possible. I have heard through all my training, try not to land. That is counterintuitive, but I am finally understanding it.

Dreaming of Future Flights

I have many more airports on my bucket list I want to visit, including Cedar Key, FL KCDK; Key West, FL KEYW; Okeechobee, FL KOBE; Saint Augustine, FL KSGJ. And those are just the ones I want to visit in Florida! I hope to expand my logbook and fly over the state line soon.

Getting into aviation and getting my pilot's license

has given me the opportunity to visit these destinations from the air, giving me a unique and exciting perspective. I look forward to visiting other airports in the future and meeting new people in the flying community for years to come.

Jackson County Sylva NC View on downwind leg

5

THE FLIGHT TRAINING

The FAA has minimum requirements for flight training. A few highlights of these requirements are below, from the Federal Aviation Regulations / Aeronautical Information Manual or FAR/AIM.

Accumulate flight experience (FAR61.109). Receive a total of 40 hr. of flight instruction and solo flight time, including

a. 20 hours of flight training from an authorized flight instructor, including at least
    1) 3 hours of cross-country, i.e., to other airports
    2) 3 hours at night, including
        a. One cross-country flight of over 100 NM total distance (Nautical Miles)
        b. 10 takeoffs and 10 landings to a full stop at an airport
    3) 3 hours of instrument flight training in an airplane
    4) 3 hours in airplanes in preparation for the practical test within 60 days prior to that test

Note: A maximum of 2.5 hours of instruction may be accomplished in an FAA-approved flight simulator or flight training device representing the airplane.

  b. 10 hours of solo flight time in an airplane, including at least
    1) 5 hours of cross-country flights
    2) One solo cross-country flight of at least 150 NM total distance, with full stop landings at a minimum of three points and with one segment of the flight consisting of a straight-line distance of more than 50 NM between the takeoff and landing locations
    3) Three solo takeoffs and landings to a full stop at an airport with an operating control tower

The above is basically a checklist of the minimum requirements in hours of training, landings, types of flight etc., to be completed in order to schedule your private pilot checkride exam with a Designated Pilot Examiner (DPE). All items will be recorded in your logbook for verification you have met the minimums.

Your training will also include preflight preparation and procedures, flying maneuvers, ground reference maneuvers, slow flight and stalls, emergency operations, postflight procedures, and much more. It is a lot to complete in 40 hours and this is why most students take 60-80 hours to complete their training.

Taking command of and becoming the pilot in control (PIC) of an airplane is a daunting and yet rewarding experience. You will learn what amounts to a completely new language, including aviation-specific terms, aviation routine weather report (METAR), and radio communications that will be unfamiliar to you at first. Simultaneously, you will learn the rules and regulations of aviation and how to maneuver and control an airplane. It takes attention to detail and Aeronautical Decision Making (ADM). Oh, and by the way, there are more acronyms than you can imagine.

Flight Training, First Hand

Gliding in an airplane is amazing. On one of our first flights, I told my instructor Jim I was a little hesitant to perform a simulated engine failure. At the time, I thought they actually turned the engine off. This procedure is basically pulling the throttle control out, which would be similar to letting off the gas in a vehicle and coasting. In an airplane, though, you aren't just coasting along, you're actually descending - or falling - out of the sky.

Jim wanted to immediately address that concern with me, so he took us to a safe altitude and pulled the power, then set the plane up for "best glide" speed. This allows the airplane to glide as far as possible in a descent and lengthens the fall from the sky.

He then let me know we had six minutes to make it to the ground. During that time, you look for the best place to make an emergency landing and begin working the plane toward that landing spot.

During the exercise, I discovered with amazement just how long six minutes is and the time I had to make calm, rational decisions. Although I certainly hope never to be in a real-life engine failure situation, I know my training prepared me should I ever find myself in that state of emergency.

What Goes Up, Must Come Down

Landing was the hardest thing for me to learn, but obviously, landing is a necessity. There are so many ever-changing variables when it comes to landing: wind direction, wind speed, other traffic that might pressure you, new airports with different reference points or narrower runways, etc.

Jim was always passionate about two things when setting up for a landing: airspeed control and the ball in the center. The turn coordinator is one of the "six pack" instruments that indicate the rate and quality of turn. There is a ball that rolls left and right indicating the roll and yaw of the airplane. It is important to keep the turn coordinated, and keeping the ball in the center will indicate you are making a coordinated turn.

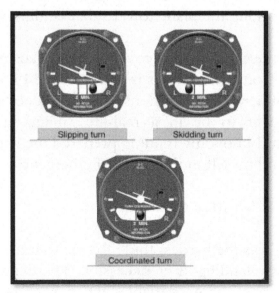

Turn Coordinator

You will hear "step on the ball" during training. This means apply pressure to the rudder where the ball is. If the ball is to the left, you would apply pressure with your foot to the left rudder pedal and the ball would move to the center. The reason for emphasizing these two things is keeping the airplane coordinated and the airspeed above stall at this critical phase of flight. The base to final turn has been a notorious place for a spiraling stall, which is the consequence of an uncoordinated turn that can have fatal consequences.

I learned to keep my pattern consistent and watch the airspeed, which has resulted in better landings.

During dual instruction, Jim taught me steep spirals. This is a fun way to get down fast. I am sure there were a few "woohoo" moments from yours truly during this exciting maneuver!

Training for Every Scenario

Emergency procedures are simulations of various scenarios such as a failed engine, a fire in the cabin, an emergency descent, and an emergency approach and landing. On one of our emergency approach and landing simulations, I really felt like we were about to land in a cow pasture. I was glad when Jim finally called for power up, so we could begin flying again.

I truly enjoyed the instrument training with foggles; imagine eyeglasses covered with only a small opening in the center near the bottom. The foggles only allow you to see your instruments with no reference to the horizon or anything outside the airplane. This is to simulate foggy conditions and limit vision. This simulation is a test of your control of the airplane without visual reference. The challenge there was flying by instrument, keeping the plane level, and changing course and/or elevation as Jim gave instruction. I enjoyed it so much I plan to train to become an instrument-rated pilot before I make it to the 200-hour mark in my logbook.

During my solo training, I used my house for turns around a point. For this maneuver, you keep an object off the tip of the wing and fly a uniform circle, varying the bank angle to account for wind effects, while maintaining a constant altitude and airspeed.

I enjoy every phase of flight and all the maneuvers with one exception: the stall. The stall is when the airplane exceeds its given critical angle of attack and is no longer able to produce lift for normal flight. The airplane will begin a descent until a recovery is made either by the pilot (preferred) or by the design of the airplane. I have gotten better, and in my biennial flight review this year, I was taught a falling leaf stall. Becoming proficient at stall recovery is necessary in flight training, but the nose up attitude and the buffeting are uncomfortable for me. The nose up attitude reduces the reference to the horizon and gives me the impression I have lost control of the airplane. As with anything, practice will help me become more proficient and less hesitant with this procedure.

Lessons Learned and Wisdom Shared

As mentioned in Chapter 3, I wish I had made better use of my solo training to become a more proficient pilot and be better prepared for my checkride. I spent most of my flight time sightseeing, and only landed when I had to get down out of necessity. In hindsight, I should have been practicing landings alone without the guidance of and dependence upon my instructor.

So, please, use the syllabus that comes with your ground school training and use your training flights for intentional practice. I'm not saying not to have fun and do some sightseeing while you're in solo training, but don't forget the mission and practice maneuvers and landings. You will have plenty of time for fun and sightseeing after you become a private pilot!

Beautiful cloud view during flight training

6

THE GROUND SCHOOL

Expect More Than Just Flying

In order to become a pilot, in addition to actually flying, you must also learn how to use radios and sectional charts, flight planning, get an understanding of airspace, federal aviation regulations, aeromedical factors, aviation weather, and the list goes on. Much of this training will be through reading books and online training.

The flight training at Bartow Flying Service came with a Gleim Private Pilot Kit with Online Ground School included. This is a very popular kit and has everything you need to pass your FAA Pilot Knowledge Test. The Gleim kit is also available for purchase on the Gleim Aviation website.

I studied the ground school materials several hours per week in the evenings, in conjunction with my weekly flight training. This approach gave me time for real-life application of the lessons I was reading and studying.

Alternatively, some pilots complete ground school

and the FAA Pilot Knowledge Test prior to beginning flight training. This is a personal decision, of course. As the student-in-command, you need to do whatever is best for your style of learning.

The FAA has a requirement that the practical test or checkride must be completed within 24 months of passing the FAA Pilot Knowledge Test, so you will want to schedule your flight training accordingly. Otherwise, you risk having to repeat the FAA Pilot Knowledge Test.

Ground School Materials - An Overview

The Gleim kit I used contained all the information necessary to pass the knowledge test. It is a comprehensive ground school resource, and the syllabus included is a wonderful means to track, document, and schedule training requirements. I only wish I had followed the recommendations more closely. I left my training plans solely to my instructor and didn't have a clear vision for what I wanted to achieve with each lesson. For future flight training, I will develop a system to debrief my last lesson and create written goals for the next, using a syllabus as a guideline.

I supplemented the Gleim kit with an online

ground school offered by MzeroA, a paid monthly subscription ground school providing access to many training videos online. In addition to the training videos, MzeroA also offers practice exams. Once you successfully pass the practice exam, you'll be able to print your required endorsement allowing you to sit for the FAA Pilot Knowledge Test.

I only needed the subscription two months, as I was able to successfully complete my practice exam within that time. Jason Schappert, the owner of MzeroA and the star of the training videos, likes to say, "A good pilot is always learning." You may decide to continue the subscription even after you pass your exam, maintaining your access to the plethora of training videos there.

The Gleim kit has great books from which I read and learned, but, in my opinion, their computer courses lacked modern graphics and high video quality at the time I took my course. At times, I would have my Gleim books in my lap or at my desk for reference while I watched the videos from MzeroA. Both tools were beneficial to my education and preparation for the knowledge test.

There are many other great companies offering

ground school/exam preparation. Do your research and determine the best school, or combination of schools, to meet your needs.

Testing Your Knowledge

The FAA contracts with two computer testing services to administer FAA knowledge tests: CATS and PSI. Both have testing centers throughout the country. You will need to find one in your area to schedule your knowledge test.

I passed my knowledge test at Sunstate Aviation in Kissimmee, FL, about an hour away from where I live, on Sept. 1, 2016. According to my logbook, I had about 20 hours of flight time at the time I sat for the exam. I was flying and taking ground school concurrently, which I think helped me better understand and apply what I was learning. I like to say I should have been born in Missouri, "The Show Me State." I learn best when I am shown how to do something, compared to reading alone.

The exam is comprised primarily of multiple-choice questions, with a few requiring use of a navigational plotter, approved flight computer, and/or pocket calculator. Those were some of my favorite questions, because I really enjoy flight planning and how science and math are utilized to calculate distance, fuel consumption and other important considerations for a successful flight or even a "no-go."

A "go or no-go" decision is based upon environmental conditions and the pilot's experience to make the judgment as to whether the flight should be completed.

Although ground school isn't as fun as flying, it is certainly a critical part of flight instruction. I am amazed at how organized and standardized the Federal Aviation Regulations are. The thought that has gone into airspace and airport procedures has definitely been good for the safety of the flying community.

As with any regulations, the rules are meant for safety. They are in place to protect pilots and the general public. Every FAA employee I have met has been either a pilot themselves or a fan of aviation. They are here to help general aviation and work to make flying safer for everyone.

7

THE SOLO

The solo flight is a monumental milestone in flight instruction with traditions and celebrations for all who experience this wonderful achievement.

The Federal Aviation Regulations Aeronautical Information Manual (FAR/AIM) Section 61.87: Solo requirements for student pilots has two and a half pages of requirements in small print that need to be met in order for a student to be the pilot in command as the sole occupant. Your instructor is tasked with ensuring you have met the requirements to take your solo flight. To me, this is like seeing your child off on their first drive alone after getting their driver's license – a heady mix of pride and anxiety. The instructor must have hesitations and reservations to release a student and let them fly, but they must trust they have been trained to handle a variety of situations.

Of course, a solo flight is the only way to become a pilot in command and be able to operate an airplane on your own, so the day of your solo flight will and must come. All pilots have successfully completed their solo at some point, and you can do it, too!

When Are You Ready?

If you Google "time required to solo," you will find a wide range of results from 10 to 30 hours of flight time. One article in AOPA Flight Training magazine, "When Will I Solo? Answers to the Age-Old Question" by LeRoy Cook, quotes an instructor having student pilots solo at six hours and others at 40 hours of flight time. Therefore, there is no set time requirement or even standard recommendation for a solo. Your instructor will let you solo when he or she believes you are ready.

Most pilots I know were trained years ago at a time when it wasn't uncommon to solo at eight hours or less. When I discussed flight training with them, they often asked how many hours I had. After I had completed 12 to 15 hours, a few of them were disappointed I had not already soloed. Being a driven person, their disappointment made me want to solo soon to meet their perceived expectations.

I began to get frustrated I wasn't ready after 15 hours of flight. At around 18 to 19 hours, when Jim told me to get ready to solo soon, I became excited and anxious. Right when I felt I was ready, I would make a mistake on landing and could feel Jim's frustration that just as he was ready to let his child go and fly free, I weakened both his and my confidence.

A Time-Honored Tradition and Getting Set for Solo

One of the celebratory traditions of flight training is to cut off the tail of your shirt after you make your solo flight. This tradition came about before radio communications, when the instructor sat behind the student. To get the student's attention, the instructor would tug on the student's shirt tail. Once a student successfully completed the solo flight, they no longer needed their shirt tail to be tugged on by an instructor. Off it came!

I had bought a few breathable shirts in various colors specifically to wear during flight training, and mentioned to Jim I didn't particularly like the baby blue one and would prefer it be the one cut off. On Sept. 6, 2016, Jim told me to wear my baby blue shirt in two days for our next scheduled training. I was at 23.2 hours of flight time. Oh, boy, was I excited. WOOHOO!

Upon arrival at the airport, after surveying the conditions, we both decided the winds were a little strong for a student solo, so we continued dual flight instruction for 1.5 hours. He told me I was definitely ready and we checked the predicted weather for the next day, Friday, Sept. 9, 2016.

My solo was scheduled.

I went home and asked my wife to wash the blue shirt for the next day. I live in the south, and even though these shirts breathe, a big guy like me just melts in the Florida heat.

I probably didn't sleep much that night. This is a very exciting time for a student pilot.

A student solo flight consists of three take-offs and landings. Friday morning, Jim and I made a few trips flying around the pattern with touch and go landings. Then he told me to take him to the FBO and drop him off. Once there, we had a briefing, he encouraged me, and I taxied off to runway 9. I stopped in the run-up area and completed my checklist, said a prayer, and then radioed the tower.

This was an adrenaline-filled moment, both exciting and daunting. I remember going from being convinced I was ready and frustrated I had not soloed yet, to wondering if I could really do this on my own.

My Solo: A Play-By-Play

Bartow is a towered airport, so radio communication is restricted to pilots and the tower. In order to support me, Jim had both the second radio in the airplane and his handheld radio set to a frequency where I could hear him but couldn't respond. This allowed him to encourage and instruct me from the ground.

Me: "Bartow Tower, Cessna 28 Zulu is holding short runway 9, would like to remain in the pattern."

Tower: "Cessna 28 Zulu clear for takeoff runway 9, make left traffic."

Me: "Clear for takeoff Runway 9, make left traffic."

"OK, here we go," I thought, and checked the final to be sure there wasn't another plane landing unannounced. Jim always told me if the control tower makes a mistake, they still go home, so always double check as if your life depends on it – because it does.

Next up, I talked myself through the steps. "Full power, let's go, apply rudder to stay on centerline of the runway, airspeed alive, oil pressure and oil temperature good. Rotation speed, gently pull the yoke back and leave the runway." I had a huge grin on my face - I was flying an airplane by myself for the first time!

At the midfield, I radioed the tower and let them know I would be landing runway 9 and they cleared me to land. I looked over to the right seat and reality set in: I have to land this airplane all by myself as the PIC.

At the runway numbers in line with the pilot's window, I pulled back the power to begin my descent, airspeed set for first notch of flaps. I glanced over my shoulder to find the correct distance for my base turn. This is approximately a 45-degree angle from the runway numbers to the middle of the airplane. I turned for base.

During the descent, I kept the rate of descent between 300-500 feet of descent per minute by watching the vertical speed indicator, keeping the ball in the middle and watching my airspeed. I lowered the flaps to the second notch.

Everything was going well. I checked the final to

be sure no other plane was coming on final. Again, always double check.

I made my final turn to line up with the runway and lowered my last notch of flaps. Everything looked good.

My first landing was a "greaser" – a smooth, textbook landing. Another huge smile had the corner of my lips trying to touch my ears!

Unfortunately, that was a short-lived moment, as it was time to focus on doing it again – twice. I applied full power for my second takeoff, airspeed alive, waiting for the rotation speed.

Oh, no! Something was wrong! I was at full power and not getting speed. As I looked down to determine what was wrong, my head was on a swivel trying to find the problem, wasting precious seconds to abort the takeoff.

When I looked back up, I felt like I was staring at the grass and had no idea what to do. I was in a complete panic! At that very moment, Jim came over the radio and instructed me to pull up.

I followed his instruction and the plane left the runway with a very rattled and nervous student pilot. He informed me over the radio that I left my flaps down. In haste and error, I pulled the flaps completely up at once. This is supposed to be done in increments as you have a positive rate of climb.

This was my second mistake. The plane would barely climb and I was getting concerned. When I finally got to traffic pattern altitude, I was midfield of the runway and requested a full stop landing. The tower gave me clearance for a full stop landing and Jim came over the radio to remind me I had to make three take-offs and landings to meet the requirements of a solo flight. I exercised my role as PIC and made a second radio announcement for a full stop landing.

This landing was good and I was laser focused after being rattled. I taxied to the FBO to have a discussion and debriefing with Jim before I completed my last takeoff and landing.

After getting an understanding of what I did wrong, I taxied back out to the runway for my final takeoff and landing, which were both textbook and without incident.

I was met at the plane by Jim, who was recording a video of me, his newly soloed trainee with a huge smile. Many of the FBO employees came out to congratulate me, and Jim cut the tail off my baby blue shirt. I had now entered the ranks of those who have soloed an airplane. It is an awesome experience that will be with me throughout my life.

A Quick Word on Spreading the Word

When to tell others about your pursuit of flight training is a personal decision each student pilot should make with careful consideration. At this point of training, I had purposefully only told my wife, children, and friends who are pilots about flight training. I wanted to get the solo complete prior to informing others.

There were two reasons for this:

1. I didn't want to make everyone aware if, for some reason, I had to stop training.
2. I didn't want everyone's opinion of flight training to muddle my experience.

I was very excited to let my friends and extended family know I was going to become a pilot after I had soloed an airplane. I was well on my way, with more fun ahead!

8

THE SOLO TRAINING

My first chance to leave the airport on my own – for more than just my triple take-off/landing solo exercise – was Sept. 15, 2016. Jim and I did a little less than half an hour of dual instruction, and then he told me to drop him off at the FBO and go have some fun.

It was my second solo flight and it was exhilarating to go out as PIC, having the control and responsibility of flying an airplane alone and deciding where to go and what to do. I chose to go out over what we call the practice area east of Bartow Airport. This flight path takes you over the Chain of Lakes in Winter Haven, past LEGOLAND and over Bok Tower Gardens in Lake Wales.

This is a beautiful area and there are many things to see while flying over. I was smiling and taking it all in, scanning for other airplanes and having a wonderful time. I really could not believe I was working toward a lifelong dream and have now flown an airplane out and about sightseeing. But I can't stay up in the air forever, so eventually I headed back to the airport.

I listened to the weather on the radio ATIS frequency. This is a required procedure to find the current weather at the airport where you are landing before you call the tower. I called the tower at Bartow and let them know I had the current weather information and would like to have a full stop landing.

The tower instructed me to make a call when I am within five miles of the airport. I made the call as instructed and was given runway 9 clear to land. I entered the downwind for runway 9 and configured the plane to land. As I came in for final, I realized I was too high and requested a "go around" to make a second attempt to land.

The tower cleared me to do a "go around" and informed me that the winds changed and I would need to make a left base for runway 23. This runway is less than a 90-degree turn, something I had not experienced to date. Given this, I was unable to configure the plane correctly in time for a landing. The airport was a bit busy and I was a little frazzled, so I request to go back to the practice area to get my wits.

I spent a little time in the practice area and

requested attempt three to land, and was instructed to enter a right base for runway 27R. When I got back to the airport, I set up to turn right for a left base for runway 27R.

That's when it dawned on me that I got confused and turned right for a left base. Once I realized my mistake, I asked the control tower for a "go around" so I can have a full pattern, which would give me time to configure the plane for the approach for which I most trained.

The tower informed me he did not know what I was requesting. Knowing this controller, I was sure he knew what I meant but was trying to teach me proper radio communication. At the moment I wanted to hurt him because I was feeling stuck in the air, unable to land.

I again exercised my role as PIC and set myself up for a full pattern for runway 27R - I had to get down. The controller then came over the radio, "28 Zulu, I see you are on the downwind for 27R, clear to land 27R."

I was going to land this time whether it was pretty or not. Jim always told me that a good landing is one you can walk away from, but a great landing is one you can walk away from and still use the plane.

This one was a great landing. In fact, all my landings (over 300 to date) have been great if that is the standard!

The Training Continues

I had several uneventful flights and training sessions with Jim after this flight. On a rainy day I had scheduled for flying, I decided to use the scheduled time to try out a flight simulator, as this training can be counted as flight instruction.

There are benefits to performing stall and spin recovery training in the simulator, since you can concentrate on response and not fear. I will say, however, the rudder pedals don't have the resistance of a real airplane and holding centerline was difficult.

Oct. 25, 2016, I took a solo flight and flew over my office, house, and a few of the power plants at which my company works. It is really cool to pick out things you recognize from the ground and get a bird's eye view. I have some great photos of my house and property, the fabrication shop where I work, and several of the jobsites in my collection of flying photos. It's also fun to wave the wings at family, friends, and co-workers.

On my Oct. 25, 2016 flight, I came back from the west and, after the weather check and call to the tower, I was given runway 9 for a straight-in landing. Visually locating an airport is difficult from the sky and this was my first solo flight coming in from the west. I finally made out the airport and the runway and lined up for a straight in landing.

After my previous difficulty with getting configured without a full pattern, I realized I needed to be at the proper elevation and configured for the landing in whatever part of the pattern I was assigned. This means, if asked to enter the base leg, I need to be lower than I would be "at the numbers." The numbers are painted on the runway indicating the runway number, and "at the numbers" means the pilot's shoulder is in line with the runway parallel with the airplane, on the downwind, because you are eliminating that leg of the pattern. If assigned a straight in, the pilot should begin descent to get to the right elevation for final since they will be entering that leg of the pattern.

This will make more sense to you once you understand the pattern, which is an imaginary rectangle around the perimeter of the airport and in line with the runway.

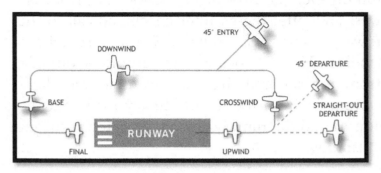

The Pattern

You take off against the wind on the runway, known as the upwind leg of the pattern. You turn crosswind at 90 degrees while continuing to climb to the traffic pattern altitude. The next step is to make a 90-degree turn down wind. At this point, you should be at traffic pattern altitude, typically 1,000 feet above runway elevation. Once you get abeam or in line with the runway numbers, looking over your shoulder for the runway from which you took off, you will begin to configure the airplane for a descent to land. The next turn is another 90-degree turn called the base turn, and the last turn is called the final, in line with the runway completing the rectangle.

That very simple explanation will get more detailed in training.

Now back to the flight. I was lined up for the runway and was configured for a straight-in approach. I focused on the runway and made a good landing. While I was slowing the plane on the runway, I got a call from the tower: "28 Zulu, do you realize you just landed on the wrong runway?"

I glanced around to get my bearing straight and sure enough, I was on runway 5 instead of runway 9. This was not a WOOHOO moment; this was a major WHOOPS moment.

I should have seen the large runway number on final and I should have verified my heading indicator for runway 9. These were two failed opportunities to verify I was on the correct runway as assigned.

I quickly realized the potential hazards associated with this error and took a big gulp. Multiple runways at an airport can be in use simultaneously, and if you are on the wrong runway, you may be an interference and have a collision with another airplane. I was given taxi instructions to the FBO. Once in the FBO, I was informed the tower wanted me to call them. I called and was given some instruction and told to contact my instructor to get further training on runways and runway incursions.

I contacted Jim to let him know I needed some additional training. Jim met me at the FBO and replicated the runways at Bartow using duct tape on the carpet in the floor of the conference room.

This training was very simple and easy to understand. He even had me walk the pattern. He would then act as if he was the tower and give me instructions to follow. It's been over two years since that flight and subsequent lesson, and the last time I was in the conference room there, the duct tape was still on the floor, hopefully helping other "show me" students.

I share these "lessons learned" with you hoping you won't make the same mistakes, but also to realize mistakes will be made and you must learn from them and move on. Don't let your mistakes define who you are.

9

THE CROSS-COUNTRY

A cross-country flight is very rewarding, in terms of both planning and sightseeing. It is similar to planning a vacation where you have a feel for the experience before you get started. Seeing your plan come to fruition is quite gratifying and rewarding!

According to the FAR/AIM, a cross-country flight involves the use of dead reckoning, pilotage, electronic navigation aids, radio aids, or other navigation systems to navigate to a landing point. It must include a point of landing that is a straight-line distance of at least 50 nautical miles from the point of departure.

My first cross-country flight was with Jim to Venice, KVNC, 63 nautical miles from KBOW. It is a beautiful flight over farmland, cattle ranches, and the beach. KVNC is a non-towered airport, or a pilot-controlled airspace.

Planning and Adjusting for Cross-Country Flight

When planning for your cross-country flight, you

will use a sectional chart, navigational plotter, and flight computer. This is where the science of flight comes in to play. You will compute the distance, fuel usage, airspeed versus ground speed, and time required for flight.

You will also have to add that ever-present variable: wind. You may have a crosswind, head wind, or tailwind that affect your calculations and impact your flight planning.

A tailwind helps you gain speed and use less fuel while a headwind has the reverse effect or slowing you down and utilizing more fuel. You may get a headwind traveling to your destination and a tailwind or crosswind departing. All these variables will affect your flight plan.

In the event of a crosswind, you must input a wind correction angle into the wind for your ground course to be correct. During flight planning, you will have picked out visual checkpoints to confirm you are on the correct course and are arriving to these checkpoints within the calculated amount of time. The checkpoints are critical in verifying everything is going as planned and you are on course and on time. The checkpoints should be unique and large enough to see from the air.

Should you discover you are off in either distance (blown off course) or in time, you should determine what caused your calculations to be inaccurate. Are you flying at the planned airspeed? Is there a difference in the actual wind (direction or speed) versus what was planned? These and other questions can help you understand and correct accordingly.

All these elements are critical to ensuring you have sufficient fuel to complete the mission. You will also need to plan for landing at alternate airports should you need to divert due to weather or an inflight emergency.

Solo Cross-Country Prep

My second cross-country flight was in preparation for my solo cross-country, where a pilot must not only fly a minimum of 50 nautical miles, but also add a third airport to create a triangle.

Jim and I chose Ocala KOCF as the first leg of the cross-country and then a stop in Lakeland KLAL, home of SUN 'n FUN Fly-In, then back to Bartow KBOW. Jim confirmed my flight plan and we scheduled the trial run flight for Nov. 21, 2016, and the subsequent cross-country solo flight for the following day.

Jim wound up being unavailable, so I flew with another instructor, Manny. Remember, having a back-up instructor is a good thing! Manny flew with me for my trial run to become familiar with the cross-country flight prior to my cross-country solo.

I invited my son, Matthew, along for the trial run. Unfortunately, I forgot to borrow an additional headset, so he was unable to communicate with us, but he enjoyed sightseeing and flying.

Manny introduced me to flight following, a wonderful air traffic advisory service provided by the FAA, in which you maintain contact with the appropriate control center until they pass you along to the next control center while keeping you clear of other air traffic.

It was amazing to me when they called out another airplane. We would struggle to find it visually, and then it would suddenly appear in view. I would most likely not see or be aware of some traffic without their assistance, making it a valuable service.

As we approached my checkpoints, I remember telling Manny we were a little early. He questioned me, asking, "Are we over the checkpoint yet?" We would continue the flight, move over the checkpoint, and be very close to the planned time. Remember, it's not when you see the checkpoint, it's when you are over it! It is reassuring to have a plan and have it work out very closely to what you calculated.

A note on checkpoints: I am very familiar with Florida and have worked at numerous power plants throughout the state, so, for me, they make wonderful checkpoints. Choose checkpoints that are easy to distinguish and will be noticeable to you.

My Solo Cross-Country Flights: Feeling Real

Nov. 22, 2016, I took my cross-country solo flight, utilizing the previous flight plan with a few tweaks for minor wind difference and a little less weight without an instructor and a son.

After departure from KBOW, I contacted flight following and they immediately gave me a west heading. I was flying toward Tampa and flew over a large phosphate gypsum stack in Plant City. I was starting to get concerned when the controller finally gave me a north heading. It was perfectly in line with Ocala, KOCF for a straight-in landing.

I landed at KOCF and felt like a "real pilot." I had the Sheltair Aviation Services employee sign my logbook to show I had made it, and then went into the restaurant to have a Coke.

As I sat in the lobby of the FBO, a commercial pilot of a King Air charter plane came up to me and asked, "What are you up to?" I must have had that accomplished student look on my face. I told him I was on my cross-country solo and he said with a smile, "I thought so." He sat down and shared with me some funny stories about his days as a commercial flight instructor.

One story he told involved a student pilot who had to make an emergency landing on a farm in north Florida. He was successful in the landing and went to the local farmer's house where, in broken English, he told the farmer and his wife he had crashed an airplane. He was wearing the school uniform of a commercial pilot. The farmer's wife called 911 to report a downed airliner. Concerned it was a passenger jet, emergency crews rolled out to respond to a downed single engine general aviation airplane. I just love flight stories – especially ones that end with everyone still healthy!

I said goodbye to my new friend and flew to

Lakeland, KLAL for a touch and go to complete the second leg of the flight. On my approach to the airport, I informed the control tower I was a student pilot. Jim has encouraged me to use the student pilot designation so the tower will understand my experience and have more patience with me. On this occasion, it worked in my favor: after clearing me to land, the controller had second thoughts and asked, "Did you say you were a student pilot?" I confirmed and he asked me to extend my downwind to allow a faster plane to land ahead of me. This reduced the pressure of an expedited landing, which could have been overwhelming for a student pilot on their first cross-country solo flight.

At Lakeland I experienced my first and, to date, only "porpoise" or "bounced" landing. A porpoise landing is where the plane lands with a high sink rate and the pilot will instinctively pull back on the yoke as you quickly approach the ground. This creates enough lift to propel the plane back into the air. I bounced twice and was able to recover the landing.

My final leg was back to the home airport Bartow, KBOW. Bartow and Lakeland are very close to each other and as soon as you climb to the traffic pattern altitude at KLAL, it is time to call KBOW control tower and let them know you are arriving. I made a smooth landing at KBOW and felt accomplished having completed my first Solo Cross-Country flight.

My next cross-country I was with Jim again, flying to Venice, KVNC at night to meet the night cross-country flight requirements. Jim emphasized to me that night flight over large bodies of water can become instrument-only flights due to the loss of the horizon. The perception at night is different and you lose some of your sight reference for landing. The landing light is good for viewing straight ahead, but you lose some of your peripheral vision and this creates a different perception you have to get used to for landing.

Overall, I really enjoy cross-country flying. This has been my ultimate motivation for learning to fly, so I can go to new places, see new things, and meet new people.

10

THE CHECKRIDE

The FAA Practical Test (commonly known as the checkride) is the final exam an aspiring pilot must complete to receive their license. This test includes an oral test of the pilot's knowledge of airspace, navigation, and emergency procedures, plus testing the pilot's competency and skills flying the airplane. The practical test must be administered by a Designated Pilot Examiner or DPE.

Requirements Complete, Anticipation Mounts

By Dec. 7, 2016, I had completed the specified requirements to schedule my checkride. I had satisfied all the requirements as described in Chapter 5 and felt prepared to schedule my test.

I was at 51.7 hours of training, including more dual training than I had planned. I was over budget and funds were running low. I told Jim my training budget was in the red and I needed to get my checkride scheduled soon. Jim contacted a DPE, with whom he had worked with for some time, to schedule my checkride.

While waiting for the DPE to contact him and confirm my checkride, Jim wanted to fly a few more instruction flights. I had several skills review flights with Jim and I also flew with the chief flight instructor at Bartow. We were all in agreement: I was ready.

It was taking a while to get scheduled for the test, and I was getting impatient. I also began to question myself; was Jim purposefully delaying the test because he didn't think I was completely ready?

Jim invited me to a pilot's safety event at the Central Florida Flying Club in early January 2017. We met a DPE at this event who was a guest speaker. I asked Jim if we could schedule him for my checkride and he agreed to ask him.

He agreed to test me, and my checkride was scheduled for Jan. 16, 2017. "WOOHOO!" I thought, "I finally get to take the exam to become a pilot!" By that point, I had a few more checkride preparation flights in my logbook and my total hours priors to checkride were 61.1 hours.

Time for My Test

Monday, Jan. 16, 2017, I met the DPE and went

over my logbook to verify all the requirements of training had been met. I actually had an excel spreadsheet color-coded by cell for each requirement with a corresponding colored tab in my logbook to find the page where the information for that requirement could be found. Night hours were orange, simulated hood hours were green, cross-country was yellow, etc. The DPE was pleased with how I had it organized and we quickly moved on to the oral examination.

If you would like a copy of this excel spreadsheet, please email me: brianb@buildcs.net.

Based on what I had read about and heard from others, I was prepared for a one-hour oral examination with numerous scenario-based questions. One scenario I remember was, if you had a sprained ankle and your friend scheduled you to fly him to an important meeting, would you press on and make the flight even with a sprained ankle? My answer was no. The DPE pressed on and said, "But you promised him you would and you scheduled it in advance. He is depending upon you to make this meeting. It is just a sprained ankle. Are you sure you wouldn't make the flight?"

I gave it some thought, trying to figure out if it was a trick question, then said, "No, if my ankle is sprained, I won't have good rudder control and I am not safe to fly." The DPE told me that was the correct answer and we moved on.

The night before the flight, the DPE had given me a destination and I had to create the flight plan based upon it. There were questions about the flight plan I had developed from that. We continued on with questions on airplane systems, airspace, radio communications, etc.

Just as I was getting weary with all the questions, he finally said, "That concludes the oral examination." I was so overwhelmed I asked if I had passed, and if we were going to be able to continue the exam. He said I had passed and we would take a flight.

We took a quick bathroom break and, while I was getting the plane checked out from the front desk, the representative, who I knew very well from my training, asked, "Are you just now getting out of the oral examination? You have been in there for two hours!"

"Yes, ma'am," I said, "I thought we had been in there for a while!"

We began with a short field take off and then

started our flight to Fort Myers, KFMY. There were a few more questions, as the oral exam can continue in flight, and then he informed me (as a simulation) that I had low oil pressure and high oil temperature. "What should you do?" he asked.

I asked if I still had an engine, and he said yes, but it had low oil pressure and high oil temperature. I decided to divert to the closest airport, which was Wauchula, KCHN. We diverted to KCHN and he told me I passed that portion of the exam. He then instructed me to make a short field landing at KCHN.

I lined up with the runway. It was my first visit to KCHN and I was a little nervous. I came in a little fast and we floated. We landed, but it didn't meet the requirements for short field.

He kindly instructed me not to be nervous and to try again. He wanted a soft field take-off, so I did as instructed. We had a very clean, soft field take-off.

We made a loop around the pattern and I made my second attempt at a short field landing. I came in fast again and he actually took the controls because he anticipated a nose wheel landing. I knew this was not good.

Deflated, But Not Deterred

We stopped in the taxiway and he told me I failed that portion of the exam. He informed me we could continue the other portions of the exam, but I would have to reschedule that portion. Basically, he gave me the option to continue with other portions or reschedule the balance of the exam. I am very deflated and don't think I would be stellar for the other portions of the exam, so I decide to reschedule the balance of the exam.

On the flight back to Bartow, he gave me several tips and pointers. A DPE is not allowed to instruct during the exam, but since I had deferred the exam, he was at liberty to give me some instruction. He was sincere and told me he wanted me to be a safe pilot and to have control of the airplane when I flew my family and friends.

In the parking lot at Bartow, he debriefed me on all the portions of the exam I had passed and the portion I had failed and gave me my Notice of Disapproval of Application, the FAA form for failing a checkride.

That was a long ride home. I was disappointed, frustrated, and questioning if I was capable of becoming a pilot. I went from thinking I was the king of the mountain to being a pebble rolling down the hill. I was able to work through my emotions, thankfully, and got my resolve in order. I started working on my recovery plan.

Getting Back in the Cockpit

I was devastated after failing my first attempt at the checkride. After some careful reflection, I determined I should have made better use of my time during both dual instruction and solo training. When you are with an instructor, just their vocal commands or the light assistance on the yoke can help you with your landings. During the examination, there is no one there to give you slight hints to improve a short field landing. I was determined to gain control of the airplane and not depend upon an instructor, since they would not be with me during the checkride.

I had seen advertised and considered a course called the Landing Bootcamp offered by Gold Standard Aviation based in Miami. I contacted them and scheduled a lesson in Miami at KOPF. This was truly a focused lesson on takeoff and landings with strong, "bootcamp-style" instructions such as:

- "Take command of this airplane."

- "Get your airspeed under control."
- "Don't let that wind whip you!"

It was intense, but beneficial for me.

I had five more flights on my own to get confidence in myself as Student in Command and focusing on solo landings. I also had two more flights with Jim concentrating on short/soft field take offs and landings. Jim had a theory that Wauchula, being a narrow runway, has a different sight picture. This may have contributed to my coming in fast, so we head to Wauchula to get more familiar with that narrow runway. Finally, I have another review with the chief flight instructor. He told me to be confident and encouraged me that I was ready.

Second Time's the Charm...?

I was very busy with my day job and, before I knew it, nearly two months flew by. This was important because the re-examination must be completed within 60 days or the student has to retake all the exam, including the oral portion and portions of the exam already passed. I didn't want to go through the whole thing again! I contacted the DPE and scheduled the re-examination for March 15, 2017, two days before the re-exam expired.

The DPE called me the night before and asked if I could manage 20-25 mile per hour wind gusts. I told him absolutely not and he wanted to know if I could reschedule the exam. I reminded him we only had two days before the re-exam expired, and he was unavailable for the days following. He told me to be at the airport earlier than planned, before the wind was supposed to get strong.

I met him at the airport and we took off and stayed in the pattern for our short field landing. I nailed it, WOOHOO! He gave me instruction for a soft field landing and, on the downwind, he commented how I have better control of my airspeed and it is like he is flying with a different pilot. Queue the big, ear-touching smile!

He then instructed me to leave the airport to complete the other parts of the exam: turns around a point, emergency landing, power on and power off stalls, etc. I am having fun and performing at my best. He finally tells me the exam is complete and to head back to the airport.

The winds are now blowing so hard it is as if the plane is hovering. I have to put in plenty of rudder for a strong crosswind and the landing isn't a "greaser," but it is good considering the current conditions. Once we cleared the runway, he said, "Congratulations, you are now a private pilot." WOOHOO!

I asked him if he has ever had a student run and jump after passing their exam. He said no, but he did have a student that, after he told him he passed, he hopped out of the running airplane, and ran into the FBO shouting, "I passed, I passed!" After he finally got back to the airplane, the DPE told him, "Well, now you have failed; we will need to reschedule." At the rescheduled exam, the DPE made the student taxi out a short distance, return to the tie down area, and follow the after-landing checklist, and then passed him. So, be sure you've completed everything required before you begin your celebration!

I was so excited that I, too, could barely contain myself. After two exam attempts, I am a private pilot! I know if I can do this, so can you!

The New Private Pilot

11

THE PASSENGERS

Souls on Board

Having a passenger is an awesome responsibility for a pilot. When a pilot has to declare an emergency, the air traffic control will ask the alarming question, "How many souls aboard?" The gravity of this question brings the pilot's awareness to its highest alert level. Being accountable for souls is a very big deal.

I usually don't invite passengers unless they have expressed an interest in flying. I want it to be their idea and I would certainly never pressure someone to fly with me.

I knew I wanted my first passenger to be special, so my wife Jennifer was my first thought. However, she didn't commit and continually gave me the "we will see" response when I brought it up during my training.

When I came home with my temporary airman certificate, it was time for Jennifer to make a decision. She finally agreed to be my first passenger and I was delighted.

A Lovely First Passenger

On March 17, 2017, Jennifer and I headed to the airport. I know I was both excited and nervous and I am sure she was, too! This was to be her first flight in a small general aviation airplane – a far cry from the passenger jets she'd flown on before.

I performed the preflight checklist and discussed the flight with her. I planned to take her over Florida Polytechnic University and then over the Ringling Bros. Center for Elephant Conservation where the famous Barnum and Bailey Circus elephants retire.

Jim and I had flown over this sanctuary a few times and it was a neat view from above. Jim always encouraged me to keep sufficient height above the sanctuary so we wouldn't disturb the elephants.

Jennifer and I were assigned runway 9 heading to the east. I requested and was granted a northeast departure to head toward Florida Polytechnic University. The company I work for erected all the aluminum architectural components that give this university its unique look and it is beautiful from the air.

Upon takeoff, Jennifer was visibly nervous. I told her we could turn around and head back to the airport, but she told me to go ahead. I could tell she was uncomfortable. A pilot doesn't want to have a nervous passenger, so I paid close attention to her as she held on to the door, obviously tense.

We flew over Winter Haven and kept a safe distance from the Winter Haven Airport. It was mid-afternoon and a little bumpy, and Jennifer was not comfortable.

Once we made it over Florida Polytechnic, she asked me to return to the airport, so we did not get to see the elephants. I resigned to save that treat for another flight. I am disappointed that she is uncomfortable, but still glad to have my wife as my first passenger.

On our return to the airport, I was constantly asking her how she was doing. Once we made final approach, she told me she was better now that the ground was outside the windshield. I explained to her the landing is the hardest part of the flight and asked, "Now you are okay?"

We had a great landing and taxied back to the FBO to return the plane to the parking area. In my logbook, I noted one half hour of flight, so it was very brief, but I was glad to have flown my first passenger on a safe flight.

Since our first together, Jennifer and I have had several more flights and she has begun to enjoy it. A few flights have been sunset flights on cool, smooth air evenings, which make for a less thrilling and more relaxing adventure.

Double the Fun on Passenger Flight Two

My twin boys were my next passengers on March 27, 2017. James and Matthew, 17 years old at the time, were very adventurous and unafraid. They have inherited that mostly from me and my father-in-law. They had both already flown with me and an instructor, so they have previous experience flying in a small plane.

I decided to take them to another airport to get a little more time and to change out seats so both of them could take a turn sitting in the front with me. We flew to Sebring KSEF.

In route, we flew over and circled Lake Clinch in Frostproof, where we've previously boated, so it was familiar to them. They enjoyed getting an aerial view.

I let Matthew take the controls and fly the plane a little over the lake. He was confident and enjoyed flying. He banked a little aggressively, so I took the controls back -- quickly.

The Sebring airspace comes close to adjoining the Avon Park Bombing range. This is a restricted flying area, so flight planning to avoid that location and being aware of the restricted times is critical.

I wasn't hearing any traffic on the radio and was concerned. When the radio is silent, there is either no traffic or the radio isn't working. I double checked the frequency and discovered I was on the wrong one.

By the time I discovered and corrected this mistake, I was on final for runway 14. As soon as I dialed in the correct frequency, I heard traffic state they were using runway 19. I let them know we were on final for runway 14 and they graciously let us land ahead of them while they did a go around.

Once on the ground, I made small talk with the pilots from that plane, who were flying a small private jet. I asked why they were using runway 19 when the wind was favoring runway 14. As an instrument pilot, he informed me he was assigned a runway by Miami Center and that the mild wind was not as critical to a jet.

During my training, instructors would tell me a pilot's license is actually a "license to learn." Knowing this, I ask questions at every opportunity, and it helps me to learn so much. On this particular flight, I learned to double check my radio frequency well before arriving at the airport. I also learned there may be unexpected runways in use.

The boys and I went into the FBO to get a soft drink and I took their photo under the Sebring Flight Center sign. Although they enjoyed flying, they did not enjoy having their picture taken. They had the "come on Dad, let's get this over" look on their faces.

We took off from Sebring and headed for home, and then I let James fly a little. He didn't like having the controls and turned them back to me pronto. I enjoyed sharing this experience with my sons and I am grateful they agreed to fly with me. It's a memory I will always cherish.

The boys have been on a few more flights with me since the first. I am glad we are able to share these flying experiences together, and I hope they catch the flying bug, just like their dad.

More Lovely Passengers Aboard

On April 13, 2017 my next passengers were my two daughters, Brittney and Rebecca, 19 and 14 years old, respectively, at the time of the flight. I knew this flight would be different from the one with their brothers when, after completing the run-up checklist, we had to pause for a selfie. No camera shyness from these two!

We took off of runway 9, heading east. Brittney had a reaction similar to that of her mother, only a little more intense. She did not like the bumpy air at all. Once we leveled off at traffic pattern altitude, she asked to return to the airport, and I obliged.

Neither of my daughters has been on another flight with me as of this writing. After consulting a few "geezers," I was encouraged not to take new passengers on discovery flights in the warm Florida afternoons. After the sun has been out for several hours, the warm rising air from the heated surface of the earth creates thermal turbulence. March is also a breezy time of year, which can add even more wind turbulence. Lesson learned! I hope to get my girls back up on a calm morning and let them experience a smooth flight. I would love nothing more than for them to get an appreciation for flying.

Another Family Flight

There was another special flight waiting for me, and I was so excited. On June 14, 2017, I got to fly my mom! She has been my inspiration for many things in life. She always encouraged my younger sister, Brandi, and me that we could do anything we put our minds to. She encouraged us and was an example for us to try new things.

While I was in Civil Air Patrol and a teenager dreaming of being a pilot, she gave me her seat on an airline flight to Atlanta -- my first commercial flight. Instead of flying to her meeting in Atlanta, she decided to allow me the flight, while she rode there with my Aunt Joy. So, as many can relate, I am indebted to and always seeking Mom's approval.

Mom asked if my niece, Madison, 16 years old at the time, could join us for the flight, and I said of course. This was to be Madison's first flight, and I was excited have Mom as a passenger and to introduce my niece to aviation.

When we arrived at the airport, it was fogged in and we were not able to fly at the scheduled time. We agreed to wait it out and the fog finally lifted for VFR (Visual Flight Rules) to apply and allow me to fly legally.

We took off from runway 9 and I circled over LEGOLAND for Madison and Mom to get a bird's eye view of the amusement park. The clouds were still a little low and it made me uncomfortable. I turned north hoping for better skies and to our intended route over Florida Polytechnic University and then to the Elephant Sanctuary. However, once we got over Winter Haven, I made the decision to turn back due to the low cloud coverage.

Madison takes a video of a "greaser" landing and in it you can hear my Mom saying, "That was great." Therefore, although it was a short flight, I had accomplished my mission and they both enjoyed the ride.

I had Madison sign my logbook and Mom added "Proud Mama flight." My ear-touching accomplishment grin appears again.

I have taken seven passengers on their first flights. I really enjoy introducing people, especially children, to flying and aviation. I have even printed a certificate to document this experience for them and have them sign my logbook.

So far, other than my girls, everyone has really enjoyed flying with me. Brittney tries to reassure me that I am a good pilot and that she just doesn't like little airplanes. I still hope to win my daughters over!

Sunset flight with Jennifer

12

THE SKEPTICS

I am a little hesitant to write this chapter, but, as an amateur 100-hour pilot, this was a concern and continuing conversation for me, and it could be for you, too. You may hear the skeptics say things like:

- "Are you crazy?"
- "I would never fly with you!"
- "That is so dangerous!"
- "I can't imagine flying an airplane."

And on and on. I even had a work acquaintance who wanted to fly with me say, "I will go with you if you promise not to kill me." I knew he was half-kidding, so I said, "To kill you in an airplane, I would have to put myself at risk, and I really don't want to kill or injure myself. So consider yourself safe!"

Misconceptions About Flight Safety

Have you ever heard it is safer to fly than it is to drive a car? I certainly had, and I even mentioned it to some of the skeptics, but it isn't entirely accurate. I found a video on the Friendly Skies Film channel entitled "How Safe is Flying?" In this video, Nick Cyganski, the producer of the Friendly Skies Film YouTube Channel and fellow general aviation pilot, does a great job of explaining the difference between flying and other modes of travel, and how we in general aviation can be safe and how to represent ourselves as such. I usually suggest this video to skeptics or those flying for the first time.

I am not suggesting flying doesn't have inherent risks, but rather that a safe pilot thinks through those risks during flight planning and makes every attempt to mitigate or eliminate the hazards to ensure a safe flight.

The checklist is one tool to utilize to mitigate or eliminate risks. I work in construction, an inherently risky and often dangerous business. We use job safety pre-briefings to reduce hazards on a jobsite and attempt to make construction jobsites less hazardous wherever possible. It is no different with aviation safety.

Root Cause Accident Analysis

Whenever I read of an aviation accident, I always

attempt to understand what happened and how it could have been prevented. Many of the accidents I've researched could have been avoided with proper planning and/or strict adherence to a checklist.

Running out of fuel is a common hazard in aviation. This is an area we can focus on as pilots and be diligent to not push on with fumes to make it to our destination. We are required to have fuel reserves and must plan to adhere to these requirements. We must check and double check our fuel consumption calculations and confirm during flight our fuel usage is going according to the flight plan. When in doubt, stop for fuel. If, during flight planning fuel shortage is even close, then go ahead and schedule a fuel stop halfway so you aren't even tempted to press on with low or no fuel.

Another deadly situation in aviation is a pilot who is VFR (visual flight rules) continuing a flight into IFR (instrument flight rules) conditions. This occurs when a VFR pilot, who should have reference to the horizon and be able to fly by sight of the ground, flies into weather that limits sight, thus necessitating instrument flying. As pilots, we should avoid flying into clouds or inclement weather through diligent planning and, if we inadvertently find ourselves in these conditions, we should turn around, making careful attempts to keep the plane level and controlled. If this is not a good option, or visibility does not increase, the pilot should declare an emergency and get help from air traffic control.

The Air Safety Institute has a video that really drives this point home entitled "178 Seconds to Live." This video, which is available on YouTube, and the statistics that inspired the title are real eye-openers and hopefully will prevent many pilots from considering moving ahead in dangerous conditions.

I encourage all pilots and aspiring pilots to take advantage of the free safety training resources provided by FAA, AOPA, EAA, etc. In this digital age, there is no excuse for not continuing education to be a safer pilot. Enroll in the FAA WINGS program and attend live events at your local airport to become a safer pilot.

News Reporting and Public Perception

Please know I am not being pious in this chapter. I have already outlined a few of my mistakes in earlier chapters, and I am sure I will have more in the future. But the greater emphasis I place on adherence to safety guidelines, the better chance my mistakes will be fewer and, hopefully, easily corrected.

Some of my family members and friends check on me whenever there is an airplane accident in our area. I am grateful they care for me and hope they never have to experience my loss or serious injury related to flying. I have encouraged them through my flying journal as follows: "In the event I suffer an aviation accident, I wish that my family and friends would grieve no differently for me than they would if I suffer an industrial or vehicle accident."

One of the problems with general aviation as it relates to public perception is the reporting and exaggeration of aviation accidents. If the excitement and attention the media uses to cover aviation accidents was similarly applied to vehicle accidents, most of us would be afraid to drive or ride in a car.

Too often, reporters make many exaggerations and errors in their reporting. I do not believe they do this maliciously, I just think they are not trained enough in aviation to report on an accident accurately.

You may hear them say, "There was no flight plan filed," as if all flights require a flight plan. While we as pilots should plan every flight, there is not always a flight plan filed or recorded for a sightseeing flight or for repetitive commute flights.

Plan for Safety as Pilot or Passenger

When you fly in general aviation, talk with the pilot and ask questions about the safety of the flight. The pilot should brief you as the passenger and hopefully make you comfortable with their planning for and commitment to a safe flight. If you are ever unsure, ask the pilot. If you are still unsure or uncomfortable after speaking with the pilot, don't take the flight.

If you are the pilot, be patient with and give more details to a nervous or new passenger and always allow them an out. Don't get your feelings hurt if they decide they don't want to fly or they don't enjoy the flight. Safety and comfort should be your top concerns when flying others.

Together, we can quiet the skeptics and keep ourselves and our passengers safe.

13

THE FLY-INS

Fly-ins are similar to airplanes and airports in that they come in various types and sizes. There are small, local fly-ins coordinated by the Experimental Aircraft Association (EAA) or other local flying clubs, on up to the largest fly-in in the United States, AirVenture in Oshkosh, WI.

The larger shows have scheduled performances by military, acrobatic, and historical performers. There is every type of aviation one could imagine - jets, biplanes, World War II relics, parachutists, gliders - all giving daily performances to the delight of the crowd. Attendees of all ages crane their necks to the sky to see these magnificent flying machines grace the air. There are also planes on display to see up close, walk through, and touch.

SUN 'n FUN in the Sunshine State

I live near Lakeland, FL, home to the EAA SUN 'n FUN Fly-In, now formally known as The SUN 'n FUN Aerospace Expo. As a Civil Air Patrol cadet in 1989, my group attended and volunteered for the SUN 'n FUN Fly-In. It remains one of my fondest memories.

Those that live in the Lakeland area become familiar with SUN 'n FUN even if they are not particularly interested in aviation. The event has a huge economic impact and draws large crowds that often create traffic jams and certainly fill the local restaurants for a few weeks.

For more than a decade, I watched the airshow from outside the airport fence, viewing what I could by looking to the skies. The annual event was a catalyst to my dream of becoming a pilot. In April of 2017, I was able to attend SUN 'n FUN not only for my first time actually entering the grounds as an adult, but as a recently licensed private pilot. WOO HOO!

I have attended every year since then and my experience at SUN 'n FUN has been wonderful as a pilot. There are exhibitors with the latest aviation technology on display, vendors selling unique aviation apparel, photography and paintings, and hands-on workshops for building and maintaining airplanes. The larger fly-ins like SUN 'n FUN have aviation seminars for pilots to learn about a plethora of subjects from pilot safety to owning and maintaining an airplane. I learn something new at each seminar, and I look forward to them every year.

The airshow pilots are amazing. Watching the military jets exhibit their flying capabilities illustrates the power of the American military and the expertise of our volunteer military pilots. Their ability to fly in precision formation and perform maneuvers only inches apart are exhilarating.

The re-enactments of historical flights and the preservation of the historical airplanes can stir up deep emotion, knowing the sacrifices others have made for our freedoms. With an interest in military history, particularly World War I and World War II, I stand in awe.

Other Outstanding Fly-Ins, and a Resource to Find Them

The AOPA has a few regional fly-ins throughout the year that don't have the airshows associated with the larger fly-ins. What they lack in scale and exhibition, though, they make up for in smaller, more intimate crowds and seminars.

I volunteered for the AOPA fly-in held in Tampa in 2018 and enjoyed meeting people and learning from other pilots. My volunteer post involved selling Chick-fil-A biscuits in a concession stand alongside a fellow local pilot. We sold chicken biscuits to a few celebrity pilots and met many wonderful people from the flying community.

On an even smaller scale and more frequent schedule are the pancake breakfast or hot dog lunch fly-ins held throughout the country. These are typically scheduled monthly. The attendees are a close-knit group, where everyone seems to know everyone else by name.

Therefore, there is a type of fly-in or expo for everyone. A great resource to be aware of planned fly-ins and other aviation events in your area (or an area that you may be traveling through) is Social Flight, an app available for download for iPhone and Android devices.

I hope to fly an airplane into Oshkosh in the future. It will be a fun challenge to understand the procedures and navigate the traffic to "land on the green dot." SUN 'n FUN has been such a wonderful experience and it is the second largest fly-in behind Oshkosh, so I can only imagine what an incredible event that must be.

14

THE GEEZERS

I learned about "Geezers" from the aviation book Flight of Passage by Rinker Buck:

"We called them the 'geezers,' the airport geezers. Every little airport in America had one or two, and still does. They're the old-timers in the Dickie pants, the matching Dickie shirt and the broad leather belt, sitting on the gas pump bench. They might be seventy or seventy-five now, not flying much anymore, but geezers aren't envious of the younger pilots, just solicitous. Geezers pour a lot of oil into hot engines and know how to squeak bugs off the windshield without wasting any cleaner. Student pilots on their first solo cross-countrys get to know the geezers quite well. It's the geezer who tells them that they have just landed at the wrong airport, and then talks to them for a while about how easy a mistake that is — all of these little airports look the same from the air — and he steers the young pilot to the right strip. Then the geezer takes the student's logbook, makes an entry for the flight and signs his name. According to him, the kid landed at the correct field."

You will discover these wise men and women of aviation wisdom hanging around every airport. Some are no longer able to fly. They may be on the FBO porch in a rocking chair or in a hangar building a home-built airplane. They are an endless source of knowledge and even some embellishments you might want to "fact check."

At a minimum, they are entertaining and usually helpful. They will be able to tell you what airplanes have flown in today and sometimes they will know (or make up) who was on them. They take jabs at each other in a light-hearted, fun banter.

They know how to fly by the seat of their pants, and they'll sure tell you how to as well. I heard one seasoned lady looking at an old Piper Cub and reminiscing about her younger days of flight and how she knew she was close to a stall when the opened and hinged window would "float."

Another time when I was rocking chair flying on the back porch of KBOW, I was listening intently to an elder talk about his cherished plane and its value. As he returned to the FBO and the door shut behind him, his fellow rocking chair flyer commented, "That piece of junk hasn't flown in years and isn't worth a thing." Then he took the opportunity to tell me about HIS cherished plane and ITS value! I guess one man's treasure is another man's junk.

There are great times to be had and lessons to be learned while hangar or rocking chair flying, and it is free of charge. The geezers can critique landings and evaluate the condition of airplanes. They seem to know the make and model of every flying machine. Of course, I have to remember those guys and gals are critiquing my landings, too. It is another motivation to make my landings better.

The geezers create a welcoming atmosphere and I have come to understand they do not mean any harm by the jabs or critiques; it is just a fun way to pass the time and enjoy aviation.

There is a saying in aviation that there are bold pilots and there are old pilots, but there aren't any bold-old pilots. As my hair continues to grey, I hope to become an old pilot and join the "geezers."

15

THE RESTAURANTS

One of the joys of being a pilot is finding the best airport restaurants to enjoy breakfast, lunch, or supper. It's the proverbial $100 hamburger, where a pilot flies to have a meal at an airport restaurant and the cost of the flight is at least $100.

You may wonder why on earth someone would spend that much money on transportation to a meal. Well, pilots need to fly to stay current and proficient with their flying skills, and adding a meal creates an opportunity to not only practice landings but also to get familiar with other airports and enjoy the flying community. Remember, the adventure is often in the journey.

There is even a book titled The $100 Hamburger that is a guide to pilots' favorite fly-in restaurants in the United States. The author, John Purner, maintains a subscription-based website regularly updated with Pilot Reports (PIREPS), on the food, fuel and services available. You can find it at www.100dollarhambuger.com.

Social Flight is a piloting app for smart phones that

details aviation events, destinations, and airport restaurants. The restaurant feature is called Burger Flights and is accessible by pressing the burger on the home screen. When using these services, be sure to verify the airport restaurant hours, as some are closed on certain days and hours change frequently.

While I was training at Bartow, KBOW, there were months of transition with no restaurant available on two occasions. The same issue has been common at Winter Haven, KGIF. As of this writing, both have really good restaurants open for business. So be sure to call the restaurant or airport before planning a visit.

My Favorite Joints

I have enjoyed meals at several of the airports in Florida. Most offer a view of the flight line. My current favorite is Runways at Bartow, KBOW. They have an excellent breakfast omelet and a to-die-for slow roasted prime rib on Friday evenings. The view of the runway is distanced, but you can see airplanes in the tiedown area and occasionally taking off.

I have also had breakfast with my wife in Sebring, KSEF. The Runway Cafe is a great restaurant and the service is exceptional.

Ocala, KOCF has Tail Winds Café where I enjoyed a Philly cheesesteak with French fries and picked up a souvenir P-51 Mustang shirt for my solo cross-country flight.

River Ranch, 2RR is a Dude Ranch Resort with a single paved runway. Visitors can rent a golf cart or walk a good distance to The Smokehouse Grill where they have a wonderful Black and Blue Cheeseburger. I hear the buffet is really good, too, but I haven't tried it for myself. It's possible to spend a day or more at River Ranch with the petting zoo, horseback riding, airboat tours, swamp buggy tours, etc. I enjoy visits there with my family.

Punta Gorda, KPGD has Skyview Café, where you can get a great breakfast, but the view of the airport is limited.

Saint Petersburg, KSPG is a great place for breakfast or lunch with an excellent view of the field. The Hangar Restaurant is located on the second story with a balcony for outdoor dining that has wonderful views of incoming and outgoing airplanes. The aviation themed décor is really nice, too.

Tampa North Aero Park, X39 has a great breakfast and lunch menu at the Happy Hanger Café. This restaurant also has a great view of the runway from the outside picnic seating area.

These are just a few of the restaurants in Florida I have had the privilege to visit. Here are a couple others that have great reputations and are on my bucket list:

- Okeechobee Executive, KOBE, The Landing Strip Café. They are well known for their breakfast.

- Venice Municipal, KVNC, Sharky's on the Pier Restaurant. My instructor, Jim, and a few other pilots have bragged about this seafood restaurant. I am thinking this will make for a nice sunset flight and dinner with my wife.

There are many opportunities to fly for a good meal and enjoy aviation. Be sure to check out the available resources and enjoy your $100 hamburger!

16

THE FLYING COMMUNITY

The flying community is an international group of pilots who respect and admire each other and their place within this tight knit, diverse group of aviation enthusiasts. When you happen to meet a fellow pilot, you have an instant bond and conversation starter. Family and friends will stand in awe of the quick connection that is made…and then be bored by the unfamiliar pilot lingo that commences!

An Early Introduction

My introduction to the flying community was as a teenage cadet enrolled in the Civil Air Patrol (CAP). The CAP is an auxiliary of The U.S. Airforce. The adults, both pilots and aviation enthusiasts, who volunteer countless hours to prepare cadets for search and rescue missions are a great example of leadership for young adults.

During my time with CAP, I learned discipline at a much-needed time in my troubled teenage years. I learned the importance of dressing sharp and taking care of yourself. It matters how you show up. I learned what a gig line was and, to this day, I still check it daily after getting dressed, that my shirt seam, belt buckle and pants seam are in line. I am grateful for my experience with CAP and highly recommend participation for young aspiring pilots.

My Friend, a Knight in the Sky

During my construction career, our company had a client that engineered and designed industrial conveying systems and contracted my company to install the conveyors and associated equipment. Bob Knight, the owner of Knight Industrial, is a pilot that utilizes his airplane, a Beechcraft Bonanza, to travel to jobsites across the country. I have had the privilege of flying with Bob on these trips on numerous occasions, and used the opportunity to discuss with him my love for aviation prior to becoming a pilot. On my twin boys' 13th birthday, I asked Bob if he would take them on their first small airplane flight. He agreed and they were smiling almost as much as I was.

Bob has served as a volunteer, board member, and even chairman of SUN 'n FUN. He has been a champion of aviation in the Lakeland community and I am privileged to have worked with him and been encouraged by him during my flight training.

On a Flight Mission

While in flight training, I would stop at various local airports in an attempt to get to know more of the flying community. On one such trip, I found Harvest Aviation, a mission that trains missionary aviation mechanics, pilots, and delivers packages and cargo to foreign missionaries. This group of mechanics, pilots, and volunteers are another example of the wonderful flying community. I was asked to become an advisor for construction projects associated with the mission expansion and am grateful to serve my small role with this outstanding group.

The mission has grown so I cannot name everyone involved today, but would like to mention those who have helped me so far:

- Chuck McConkey is a Vietnam veteran helicopter pilot and a former missionary pilot. Chuck is a joy to be around and is fun to fly with.

- Mike Burch is an airline pilot and one of the founders of Harvest Aviation. He has piloted many flights for the mission.

- Brian Smith is the chief pilot for Harvest Aviation and has become a full-time missionary pilot. I have taken lessons and gotten great pointers from Brian.

- Ronny Erekson is a full-time missionary aviation mechanic and keeps the airplanes at Harvest Aviation in good working order.

If you would like to find out more about and donate to Harvest Aviation please visit www.harvestaviation.org.

Messages from Above

Jerry Stevens is a 75-year-old skywriting pilot who writes positive messages over central Florida, often near the numerous theme parks to reach many people.

I met Jerry at KBOW and we became friends. His messages are up to seven miles long and one mile tall and can be seen from 50 miles away. They are written into the wind so that the message remains intact. I once asked him which letter is the most difficult to write in the sky and he told me it is S, because he has to fly the plane at all angles to create it.

When Jerry found out I passed my private pilot checkride, he gave me a belt with wings on it. This cherished gift I wear frequently will always be a reminder of my great friend from the flying community.

An Inspirational Flying Friend

Jessica Cox is the first armless pilot in aviation history. I became aware of her through her YouTube videos and invited her to be a guest on my leadership show, Build Your Success Podcast. Jessica agreed and we had a wonderful interview. If you are interested this is episode 16 – Embracing and Overcoming Challenges. You can find the podcast on most podcast platforms.

Jessica is a very driven person and a true inspiration. Not only is she a pilot, but she also holds a black belt in Taekwondo and is an international motivational speaker. Jessica says, and proves, that disability is not inability. I am glad to have Jessica as part of the flying community.

I haven't mentioned everyone I have met during my short time as a pilot, and I fully expect to meet many more inspiring and awesome friends who share the love of flying.

I hope you will join the flying community and get to know and be inspired by some of its wonderful people. I am not sure the Wright Brothers could have ever imagined the impact their flying machine would have on mankind, not only for air and space travel, but also for individuals to set and achieve goals that are at first daunting and then exhilarating.

Growing up, I was exposed to all kinds of interests, t-ball, baseball, football, soccer, band, church and Civil Air Patrol. My mom was hoping something would stick. I am glad that my faith, work ethic and love for flying have all stuck with me.

Safe Flying!

ABOUT THE AUTHOR

Brian Brogen is a John Maxwell Certified Coach, Teacher, and Speaker with a knack for developing teams and individuals both personally and professionally. Brian works with organizations and individuals, coaching based on his experience, knowledge, tenacity, and sense of humor, helping his clients reach their goals.

Brian leads BUILD Consulting Services (www.buildcs.net), and is the host of the Build Your Success podcast. You can reach Brian at 863-800-9658 or BrianB@buildcs.net.

Brian would like to thank Michelle Crawford of Polished Expressions for final edits and  polishing of this book. She is a great resource if you plan to publish a book or other work. You can find out more about her services at www.PolishedExpressions.com.